SPEECH,

AT THE

DINNER GIVEN IN HONOR

OF

GEORGE PEABODY, ESQ., OF LONDON,

BY THE

CITIZENS OF THE OLD TOWN OF DANVERS,

OCTOBER 9, 1856,

BY EDWARD EVERETT.

BOSTON:
PRINTED BY HENRY W. DUTTON AND SON.
1857.

SPEECH.

Mr. President:—

I suppose you have called upon me to respond to this interesting toast,* chiefly because I filled a few years ago a place abroad, which made me in some degree the associate of your distinguished guest, in the kindly office of promoting good will between the two great branches of the Anglo-Saxon or Anglo-Norman race, (for I do not think it matters much by which name you call it,) "the fair mother and the fairer daughter," to which the toast alludes. At all events, I had much opportunity, during my residence in England, to witness the honorable position of Mr. Peabody in the commercial and social circles of London; his efforts to make the citizens of the two countries favorably known to each other; and generally that course of life and conduct, which has contributed to procure him the well-deserved honors of this day, and which shows that he fully enters into the spirit of the sentiment just propounded from the chair.

To the prayer of that sentiment, Sir, I fully respond, desiring nothing more ardently in the foreign relations of the country, than that these two great nations may be rivals only in their efforts to promote the welfare and improvement of mankind. They have already done, they are now doing much, at home and abroad, to promote that end by the arts of peace. Whenever they coöperate they can sweep everything before them;—when they are at variance, when they pull opposite ways, it is the annihilation of much of the moral power of both.

---

* The following is the toast, to which Mr. Everett was called upon to reply:— "England and America, *Pulchra mater, pulchrior filia,* long may they flourish in the bonds of peace, rivals only in their efforts to civilize and christianize the world."

Whenever England and America combine their influence in promoting a worthy object, it moves forward like a vessel propelled by the united force of wind and steam; but when they are in conflict with each other, it is like the struggle of the toiling engine against the opposing tempest. It is well if the laboring vessel holds her own; there is danger if the steam prevails that she may be crowded under the mountain waves, or, if the storm gains the mastery, that she may drift upon the rocks.

It is very obvious to remark, on this occasion, and on this subject, while you are offering a tribute of respect to a distinguished man of business, that these two great nations, which are doing so much for the advancement of civilization, are the two leading commercial nations of the world; that they have carried navigation and commerce to a height unknown before. And this consideration, Sir, will serve to justify you and your fellow-citizens, if they need justification, for the honors you are bestowing upon the guest of the day, as it will the other communities in different parts of the country, which have been desirous of joining in similar public demonstrations of respect. Without wishing to disparage the services which command your respect and gratitude, in the walks of political, military, or literary life, it is natural that, in a country like the United States, where commerce is so important an interest, you should be prompt to recognize distinguished merit in the commercial career; a career of which, when pursued with diligence, sagacity, enterprise, integrity and honor, I deem it not too much to say, that it stands behind no other in its titles to respect and consideration; as I deem it not too much to say of commerce in its largest comprehension, that it has done as much in all time, and is now doing as much, to promote the general cause of civilization, as any of the other great pursuits of life.

Trace its history for a moment from the earliest period. In the infancy of the world its caravans, like gigantic silk worms, went creeping, with their innumerable legs, through the arid wastes of Asia and Africa, and bound the human family together in those vast regions as they bind it together now. Its colonial establishments scattered the Grecian culture all round the shores of the Mediterranean, and carried the adventurers of Tyre and Carthage to the north of Europe and the south of Africa. The walled cities of the middle ages prevented the arts and refinements of life from being trampled out of existence under the iron heel of the feudal powers. The Hanse Towns were the bulwark of liberty and property in the north and west of Europe for ages. The germ of the representative system sprang from the municipal franchises of the boroughs. At the revival of letters, the merchant princes of Florence received the fugitive arts of Greece into their stately palaces. The spirit of commercial adventure produced that movement in the fifteenth century which led Columbus to America, and Vasco di Gama around the Cape of Good Hope. The deep foundations of the modern system of international law were laid in the interests and rights of commerce, and the necessity of protecting them. Commerce sprinkled the treasures of the newly-found Indies throughout the western nations; it nerved the arm of civil and religious liberty in the Protestant world; it gradually extended the colonial system of Europe to the ends of the earth, and with it the elements of future independent, civilized, republican governments.

But why should we dwell on the past? What is it that gives vigor to the civilization of the present day but the world-wide extension of commercial intercourse, by which all the products of the earth and of the ocean—of the soil, the mine, the loom, and the forest—of bounteous nature, creative art, and untiring industry, are brought by the agencies of commerce into the universal market of demand and supply. No matter in what region, the desirable product is bestowed on man by a liberal Providence, or fabricated by human skill. It may clothe the hills of China with its fragrant foliage; it may glitter in the golden sands of California; it may wallow in the depths of Arctic seas; it may ripen and whiten on the fertile plains of the sunny South; it may spring forth from the flying shuttles of Manchester in England or Manchester in America—the great world-magnet of commerce attracts it all alike, and gathers it all up for the service of man. I do not speak of English commerce or American commerce. Such d'stinctions enfeeble our conceptions. I speak of commerce in the aggregate—the great ebbing and flowing tides of the commercial world—the great gulf-streams of traffic which flow round from hemisphere to hemisphere,—the mighty trade-winds of commerce which sweep from the old world to the new,—that vast aggregate system which embraces the whole family of man, and brings the overflowing treasures of nature and art into kindly relation with human want, convenience and taste.

In carrying on this system, think for a moment of the stupendous agencies that are put in motion. Think for a moment of all the ships that navigate the sea. An old Latin poet, who knew no waters beyond those of the Mediterranean and Levant, says that the man must have had a triple casing of oak and brass about his bosom, who first trusted his frail bark on the raging sea. How many thousands of vessels, laden by commerce, are at this moment navigating, not the narrow seas, frequented by the ancients, but these world encompassing oceans! Think next of the mountains of brick, and stone, and iron, built up into the great commercial cities of the world; and of all the mighty works of ancient and modern contrivance and structure,—the moles, the lighthouses, the bridges, the canals, the roads, the railways, the depth of mines, the titanic force of enginery, the delving ploughs, the scythes, the reapers, the looms, the electric telegraphs, the vehicles of all descriptions, which directly or indirectly are employed or put in motion by commerce; and last, and most important, the millions of human beings that conduct, and regulate, and combine these inanimate, organic, and mechanical forces.

And now, Sir, is it anything less than a liberal profession, which carries a quick intelligence, a prophetic forecast, an industry that never tires, and, more than all, and above all, a stainless probity beyond reproach and beyond suspicion, into this vast and complicated system, and by the blessing of Providence, works out a prosperous result? Such is the vocation of the merchant—the man of business—pursued in many departments of foreign and domestic trade—of finance, of exchange—but all comprehended under the general name of commerce; all concerned in weaving the mighty network of mutually beneficial exchanges which enwraps the world.

I know there is a shade to this bright picture: where among the works or the fortunes of men shall we find one that is all sunlight? Napoleon the First thought he had said enough to disparage England when he had pronounced her a nation of shopkeepers; and we Americans are said by some of our own writers to be slaves of the almighty dollar. But these are sallies of national hostility, or the rebukes which a stern moral sense rightly administers to the besetting sins of individuals or communities. Every pursuit in life, however, has its bright and its dark phase; every pursuit may be followed in a generous spirit for honorable ends, or in a mean, selfish, corrupt spirit, beginning and ending in personal gratification. But this is no more the case with the commercial than any other career. What more different than the profession of the law, as pursued by the upright counsellor, who spreads the shield of eternal justice over your life and fortune, and the wicked pettifogger who drags you through the thorns and brambles of vexatious litigation? What more different than the beloved physician, the sound of whose soft footstep, as he ascends your staircase, carries hope and comfort to the couch of weariness and suffering, and the solemn, palavering, impudent quack, who fattens on the fears and frailties of his victims? What more different than the pulpit which reproves, rebukes, and exhorts in the spirit and with the authority of the gospel, and the pulpit which inflames and maddens, perplexes or puts to sleep? What more different than the press, which, like the morning sun, sheds light and truth through the land, and the press which daily distils the concentrated venom of personal malice and party detraction from its dripping wings? I believe that the commercial profession is as capable of being pursued with intelligence, honor, and public spirit, as any other; and, when so pursued, is as compatible with purity, and elevation of character as any other; as well entitled to the honors which a community bestows on those who adorn and serve it; the honors which you this day delight to pay to our friend and guest.

I was not the witness of the commencement of his career abroad; but we all know that it soon fell upon that disastrous period when all American credit stood low—when the default of some of the States, the temporary inability of others to meet their obligations, and the failure of several of our moneyed institutions, threw doubt and distrust on all American securities. That great sympathetic nerve (as the anatomists call it) of the commercial world—credit—as far as the United States were concerned, was for a time paralyzed. At that moment, and it was a trying one, our friend not only stood firm himself, but he was the cause of firmness in others. There were not at the time, probably, a half a dozen other men in Europe, who, upon the subject of American securities, would have been listened to for a moment, in the parlor of the Bank of England. But his judgment commanded respect—his integrity won back the reliance which men had been accustomed to place on American securities. The reproach in which they were all indiscriminately involved was gradually wiped away, from those of a substantial character; and if on this solid basis of unsuspected good faith he reared his own prosperity, let it be remembered that, at the same time, he retrieved the credit of the State of which he was the agent; performing the miracle, if I may so venture to express myself, by which the word of an honest man turns paper into gold.

A course like this, however commendable, might proceed from calculation. If it led to prosperity and opulence it might be pursued from motives exclusively selfish. But Mr. Peabody took a different view of the matter, and immediately began to act upon an old fashioned New England maxim, which I dare say he learned in childhood and carried with him from Danvers,—that influence and property have their duties as well as their privileges. He set himself to work to promote the convenience and enhance the enjoyments of his travelling fellow countrymen—a numerous and important class. The traveller —often the friendless traveller—stands greatly in need of good offices in a foreign land. Several of you, my friends, know this, I am sure, by experience; some of you can say how perseveringly, how liberally, these good offices were extended by our friend, through a long course of years, to his travelling countrymen. How many days, otherwise weary, have been winged with cheerful enjoyments through his agency; how many otherwise dull hours in health and in sickness enlivened by his attentions!

It occurred to our friend especially to do that on a large scale, which had hitherto been done to a very limited extent by our diplomatic representatives abroad. The small salaries and still smaller private fortunes (with a single exception) of our ministers at St. James, had prevented them from extending the rites of hospitality as liberally as they could have wished to their fellow-citizens abroad. Our friend happily, with ample means, determined to supply the defect; and brought together at the social board, from year to year, at a succession of entertainments equally magnificent and tasteful, hundreds of his own countrymen and of his English friends. How much was done in this way to promote kind feeling and mutual good will, to soften prejudice, to establish a good understanding, in a word, to nurture that generous rivalry inculcated in the sentiment to which you have bid me respond, I need not say. I have been particularly requested by my friend, Sir Henry Holland, a gentleman of the highest social and professional standing, to state, while expressing his deep regret that he cannot, in conformity with your kind invitation, participate in this day's festivities, that he has attended several of Mr. Peabody's international entertainments in London, and felt them to be of the happiest tendency in promoting kind feeling between the two countries.

We are bound as Americans, on this occasion particularly, to remember the very important services rendered by your guest to his countrymen who went to England in 1851, with specimens of the products and arts of this country, to be exhibited at the Crystal Palace. In most, perhaps in all other countries, this exhibition had been made a government affair. Commissioners were appointed by authority to protect the interests of the exhibitors, and, what was more important, appropriations of money were made to defray their expenses. No appropriations were made by Congress. Our exhibitors arrived friendless, some of them penniless, in the great commercial Babel of the world. They found the portion of the Crystal Palace assigned to our country unprepared for the specimens of art and industry which they had brought with them; naked and unadorned, by the side of the neighboring arcades and galleries, fitted up with elegance and splendor by the richest governments in Europe. The English press began to launch its too ready sarcasms at the sorry appearance which brother Jonathan seemed likely to make, and all the exhibitors from this country, and all who felt an interest in their success, were disheartened. At this critical moment our friend stepped forward; he did what Congress should have done. By liberal advances on his part, the American department was fitted up; and day after day, as some new product of American ingenuity and taste was added to the list,—McCormick's reaper, Colt's revolver, Powers' Greek slave, Hobbs' unpickable lock, Hoe's wonderful printing presses, and Bond's more wonderful spring governor, it began to be suspected that Brother Jonathan was not quite so much of a simpleton as had been thought. He had contributed his full share, if not to the splendor, at least to the utilities of the exhibition. In fact the leading journal at London, with a magnanimity which did it honor, admitted that England had derived more real benefit from the contributions of the United States than from those of any other country.

But our friend, on that occasion, much as he had done in the way mentioned to promote the interests and success of the American exhibitors, and to enable them to sustain that generous rivalry to which the toast alludes, thought he had not yet done enough for their gratification. Accordingly, in a most generous international banquet, he brought together on the one hand the most prominent of his countrymen, drawn by the occasion to London, and on the other hand, the chairman of the Royal Commission, with other persons of consideration in England, and his British friends generally; and in a loving cup, made of old Danvers oak, pledged them, on both sides, to warmer feelings of mutual good will, than they had before entertained.

In these ways, Mr. President, our friend has certainly done his share to carry into effect the principle of the toast, to which you call upon me to reply. But it is not wholly nor chiefly these kindly offices and comprehensive courtesies; not the success with which he has pursued the paths of business life, nor the moral courage with which, at an alarming crisis, and the peril of his own fortunes, he sustained the credit of the State he represented—it is not these services that have called forth this demonstration of respect. Your quiet village, my friends, has not gone forth in eager throngs to meet the successful financier; the youthful voices, to which we listened with such pleasure in the morning, have not been attuned to sing the praises of the prosperous banker. No, it is the fellow-citizen who, from the arcades of the London exchange, laid up treasure in the hearts of his countrymen; the true patriot who, amidst the splendors of the old world's capital, said in his heart—If I forget thee, oh Jerusalem, let my right hand forget her cunning; if I do not remember thee let my tongue cleave to the roof of my mouth;—it is the dutiful and grateful child and benefactor of old Danvers whom you welcome back to his home.

Yes, Sir, and the property you have invested in yonder simple edifice, and in providing the means of innocent occupation for hours of leisure,—of instructing the minds and forming the intellectual character not merely of the generation now rising, but of that which shall take their places, when the heads of those dear children, who so lately passed in happy review before you, shall be as gray as mine, and of others still more distant, who shall plant kind flowers on our graves—it is the property you have laid up in this investment which will embalm your name in the blessings of posterity, when granite and marble shall crumble to dust. Moth and rust shall not corrupt it; they might as easily corrupt the pure white portals of the heavenly city, where "every several gate is of one pearl." Thieves shall not break through and steal it; they might as easily break through the vaulted sky and steal the brightest star in the firmament.

The great sententious poet has eulogized the "Man of Ross" —the man of practical, unostentatious benevolence—above all the heroes and statesmen of the Augustan Age of England. He asks—

"Who hung with woods the mountain's sultry brow?
From the dry rock, who bade the waters flow?
Not to the skies in useless columns tost,
Or in proud falls magnificently lost,
But clear and artless, pouring through the plain
Health to the sick, and solace to the swain."

But your Man of Ross, my friends, has taught a nobler stream to flow through his native village—the bubbling, sparkling, mind-refreshing, soul-cheering stream, which renews while it satisfies the generous thirst for knowledge,—that strong unquenchable thirst "which from the soul doth spring,"—which gains new eagerness from the draught that allays it, forever returning though forever slaked, to the cool deep fountains of eternal truth.

You well recollect, my Danvers friends, the 16th of June, 1852, when you assembled to celebrate the centennial anniversary of the separation of Danvers from the parent stock. Your pleasant village arrayed herself that day in her holiday robes. Her resident citizens with one accord took part in the festivities. Many of her children, dispersed through the Union, returned that day to the homestead. One long absent was wanting, whom you would gladly have seen among you. But you had not forgotten him nor he you. He was beyond the sea, absent in body, but present in spirit and in kindly remembrance. In reply to your invitation, he returned, as the custom is, a letter of acknowledgment, enclosing a sealed paper, with an endorsement setting forth that it contained Mr. Peabody's sentiment, and was not to be opened till the toasts were proposed at the public dinner. The time arrived,—the paper was opened,—and it contained the following sound and significant sentiment :—"Education,—A debt due from the present to future generations."

Now we all know that, on an occasion of this kind, a loose slip of paper, such as a sentiment is apt to be written on, is in danger of being lost; a puff of air is enough to blow it away. Accordingly, just by way of paper-weight, just to keep the toast safe on the table, and also to illustrate his view of this new way of paying old debts, Mr. Peabody laid down twenty thousand dollars on the top of his sentiment ; and for the sake of still greater security, has since added about as much more. Hence it has come to pass, that this excellent sentiment has sunk deep into the minds of our Danvers friends, and has, I suspect, mainly contributed to the honors and pleasures of this day.

But I have occupied, Mr. President, much more than my share of your time; and, on taking my seat, I will only congratulate you on this joyous occasion, as I congratulate our friend and guest at having had it in his power to surround himself with so many smiling faces and warm hearts.

www.ingramcontent.com/pod-product-compliance
Lightning Source LLC
LaVergne TN
LVHW020644110826
845149LV00004B/1344

* 9 7 8 1 4 1 8 1 8 9 7 5 4 *